W9-ASL-450

DATE DUE

Finding Patterns

City Patterns

by Nathan Olson

Capstone press

Mankato, Minnesota

A+ Books are published by Capstone Press,
151 Good Counsel Drive, P.O. Box 669, Mankato, Minnesota 56002.
www.capstonepress.com

1 2 3 4 5 6 12 11 10 09 08 07

Library of Congress Cataloging-in-Publication Data
Olson, Nathan.
   City patterns / by Nathan Olson.
   p. cm.—(A+ books. Finding patterns)
   Summary: "Simple text and color photographs introduce different kinds of patterns found in the city"—Provided by publisher.
   Includes bibliographical references and index.
   ISBN-13: 978-0-7368-6730-6 (hardcover)
   ISBN-10: 0-7368-6730-9 (hardcover)
   ISBN-13: 978-0-7368-7848-7 (softcover pbk.)
   ISBN-10: 0-7368-7848-3 (softcover pbk.)
   1. Pattern perception—Juvenile literature. 2. Cities and towns—Miscellanea—Juvenile literature. I. Title. II. Series.
BF294.O52 2007
516'.15—dc22   2006018190

Credits

Jenny Marks, editor; Renée Doyle, designer; Charlene Deyle, photo researcher; Scott Thoms, photo editor

Photo Credits

Aurora/IPN/WorldFoto/Paul Souders, 14; Capstone Press/Kay Olson, cover (buildings); Corbis/Alan Schein Photography, 12; Corbis/Angelo Hornak, 7; Corbis/Bob Krist, 18–19; Corbis/Jean-Pierre Lescourret, 8; Corbis/Kelly-Mooney Photography, 24; Corbis/Natalie Fobes, 22; Corbis/William Manning, 20–21; Corbis/zefa/Fridmar Damm, 16–17; Getty Images Inc./Photonica/Alex Maclean, 9; Getty Images Inc./Reportage/Brian Bahr, 23; Shutterstock/Anita de Vries, 6; Shutterstock/David Burrows, cover (brick), 1; Shutterstock/Johnny Lye, 26–27; Shutterstock/Lee Torrens, 11; Shutterstock/Merideth Book, 25; Shutterstock/Thorsten Rust, 29; SuperStock/age fotostock, 4–5, 10, 15; SuperStock/Mike Ford, 13

Note to Parents, Teachers, and Librarians

Finding Patterns uses color photographs and a nonfiction format to introduce readers to seeing patterns in the real world. *City Patterns* is designed to be read aloud to a pre-reader, or to be read independently by an early reader. Images and activities encourage mathematical thinking in early readers and listeners. The book encourages further learning by including the following sections: Table of Contents, City Pattern Facts, Glossary, Read More, Internet Sites, and Index. Early readers may need assistance using these features.

Table of Contents

What Is a Pattern?

A pattern is made when a color or shape repeats. Let's look for patterns all around the city.

Bricks the same size and shape pave this city street. Brick after brick makes a repeating pattern.

Stones of different sizes and shapes pave a walkway, but they do not make a pattern.

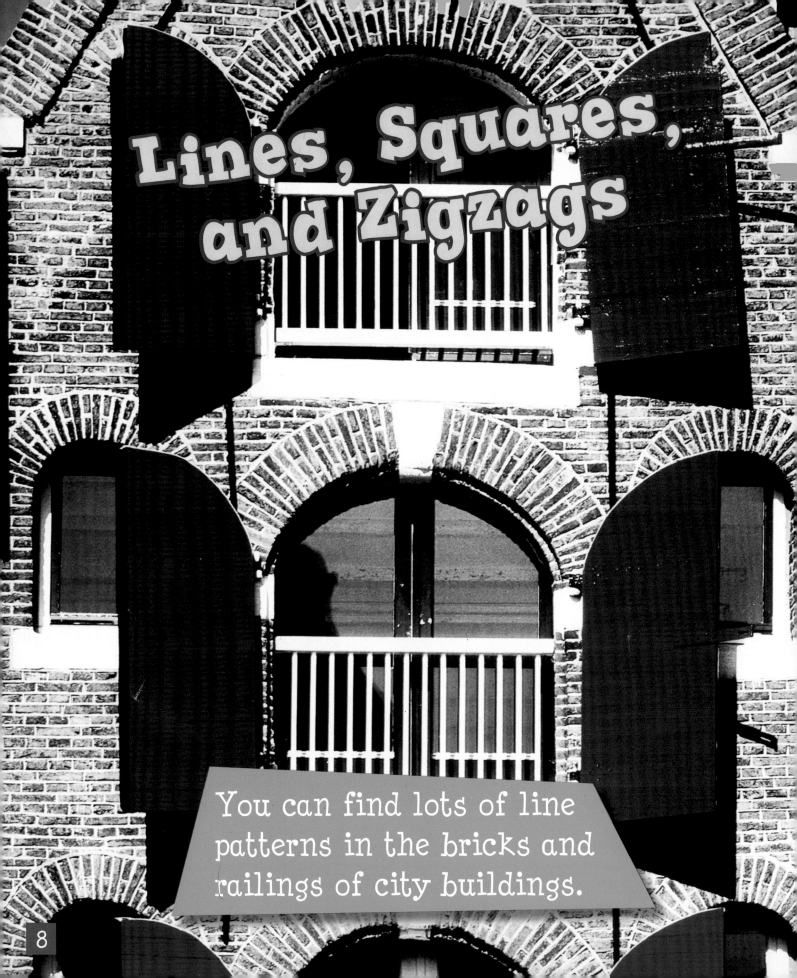

Lines, Squares, and Zigzags

You can find lots of line patterns in the bricks and railings of city buildings.

From the air, you can see other lines that repeat in neighborhoods and on city streets.

Parking meters line up, side by side, in a pattern.

A grassy green pattern of squares repeats on this city sidewalk.

Squares with repeating
every-other colors make
a checkered pattern.

Painted lines in crosswalks
make a pattern that helps you
safely cross the street.

Escalators make zigzag patterns that move people up and down inside city buildings.

A fire escape zigzags too. What other patterns do you see?

Taxicabs line up in a pattern called a queue. When you're ready for a ride, go to the head of the line.

Do you see any line, zigzag, or square patterns in this city scene?

18

Fun City Patterns

Munch your lunch under a pattern! What repeated colors and shapes do you see?

A baseball field has lots of lines, stripes, and even checkered patterns.

Marching bands make patterns that move to music.

It's fun to zip down a water park pattern. Rows of wet and wild slides repeat.

Rows aren't the only patterns that are fun to ride! The Ferris wheel's pattern fans out in all directions.

At night, city patterns burst to life high above the skyline.

City Pattern Facts

Fire escapes are stairways built outside of buildings. They are a very important pattern. The stairs are emergency exits in case of fires. City apartments and buildings need at least two exits in case of emergency.

Shutters are wooden doors that can be closed over windows. Window shutters help block out light or strong winds and rain. Can you guess how shutters got their name?

Pictures taken from the top of very tall buildings, airplanes, or even spaceships are called "birds-eye view." These types of pictures give us a view of what birds see when they are flying.

The stripes of a crosswalk are easy to see on the street. When the walkers are within the black and white striped pattern, drivers must stop and allow walkers to cross.

A checkered pattern is made up of same-size squares. The squares alternate between two colors. The name checkered comes from the game of checkers.

Skyscraper is the name given to a very tall city building. Skyscrapers are at least 500 feet (152 meters) tall. Each floor of windows usually makes a pattern.

Glossary

checkered (CHEK-uhrd)—a pattern of squares
　　that alternates between two colors

crosswalk (KRAWSS-wawk)—a place where
　　walkers can safely cross the street

escalator (ESS-kuh-lay-tur)—a moving staircase

fire escape (FIRE ess-KAPE)—a set of stairs
　　on the outside of a building that allows
　　people to escape in case of fire

pave (PAYV)—to cover a road or other surface
　　with a hard material

queue (KYOO)—a waiting line of taxicabs

skyline (SKYE-line)—the outline of buildings
　　or other objects seen against the sky
　　from a distance

walkway (WAWK-way)—a path or passage
　　for walking

zigzag (ZIG-zag)—a line or course that moves
　　in short, sharp turns or angles from one side
　　to the other

Read More

Bruce, Lisa. *Patterns in the Park.* Math All Around Me. Chicago: Raintree, 2004.

Dalton, Julie. *Patterns Everywhere.* Rookie Read-About Math. New York: Children's Press, 2005.

Hammersmith, Craig. *Patterns.* Spyglass Books. Minneapolis: Compass Point Books, 2003.

Internet Sites

FactHound offers a safe, fun way to find Internet sites related to this book. All of the sites on FactHound have been researched by our staff.

Here's how:

1. Go to www.facthound.com
2. Select your grade level.
3. Type in this book ID **0736867309** for age-appropriate sites. You may also browse subjects by clicking on the letters, or by clicking on pictures and words.
4. Click on the **Fetch It** button.

FactHound will fetch the best sites for you!

Index